ESSENTIAL LIBRARY OF
THE US MILITARY

★ THE US ★
MARINE CORPS

Essential Library

An Imprint of Abdo Publishing | www.abdopublishing.com

ESSENTIAL LIBRARY OF
THE US MILITARY

★ THE US ★
MARINE CORPS

BY REBECCA ROWELL

CONTENT CONSULTANT
MITCHELL A. YOCKELSON,
ADJUNCT FACULTY, US NAVAL ACADEMY

www.abdopublishing.com

Published by Abdo Publishing, a division of ABDO, PO Box 398166, Minneapolis,
Minnesota 55439. Copyright © 2015 by Abdo Consulting Group, Inc. International
copyrights reserved in all countries. No part of this book may be reproduced in
any form without written permission from the publisher. Essential Library™ is a
trademark and logo of Abdo Publishing.

Printed in the United States of America, North Mankato, Minnesota
042014
092014

Cover Photo: Laura K. Smith/US Air Force
Interior Photos: Laura K. Smith/US Air Force, 2; US Marine Corps, 6–7, 11, 39, 55,
56–57, 60, 64, 66, 68–69, 73, 78–79, 81, 83, 86, 90–91, 96, 100; AP Images, 13; US
Navy Art Collection, 16–17; National Archives, 20; Library of Congress, 23, 29; US
Naval Academy Museum, 24–25; Bettmann/Corbis, 32–33; Horst Fass/AP Images, 41;
Sadayuki Mikami/AP Images, 43; Dave Martin/AP Images, 46–47; Red Line Editorial,
50; Bullit Marquez/AP Images, 53; US Navy/AP Images, 77; Shutterstock Images, 93

Editor: Melissa York
Series Designer: Jake Nordby

Library of Congress Control Number: 2014932873

Cataloging-in-Publication Data

Rowell, Rebecca.
 The US Marine Corps / Rebecca Rowell.
   p. cm. -- (Essential library of the US military)
 ISBN 978-1-62403-435-0
 1. United States. Marine Corps--Juvenile literature.   I. Title.
 359.9/60973--dc23

2014932873

CONTENTS

Marines approached the island of Iwo Jima, crowned by Mount Suribachi, on February 19, 1945.

CHAPTER ONE
RAISING THE FLAG

The men headed out. Actually, they headed up. Forty marines marched up Mount Suribachi.[1] Their goal was to claim the extinct volcano for the United States. And they climbed the rugged terrain prepared to fight, armed with an assortment of weapons and ammunition.

For years, the fighting and destruction of World War II (1939–1945) had dragged on, costing millions of civilian and military lives. On June 6, 1944, Allied forces successfully invaded Normandy, France. The amphibious assault marked the beginning of a months-long effort to drive back German forces.

But the fighting of World War II also took place well beyond Europe. US and Japanese forces met in the Pacific. In the ocean's western part, a small island became the site of a hard-fought battle that would prove vital to Allied victory. Since 2007, it has been known officially as Iō-tō. History and the Americans who battled for it refer to the place by a different name: Iwo Jima.

Only eight square miles (20 sq km), Iwo Jima is the largest of Japan's three Volcano Islands. Its landscape is volcanic rock. It is desolate and lacks water. Even so, Iwo Jima appealed to US forces. Situated between the Mariana Islands and Japan, the location was valuable strategically. If US forces captured Iwo Jima, they could use the island as a base from which to launch fighter planes. If successful, the United States would do more than acquire an ideal location for military operations in its battle against Japan. It would take the island from the Japanese—the enemy—and occupy Japanese soil.

THE MARINES ARRIVE

On December 8, 1944, US planes began bombing the island. It was the beginning of a 74-day offensive. The air attacks lasted until February, when the US Marines invaded. The Fifth Amphibious Corps left the Mariana Islands February 15 and 16, 1945, heading north hundreds of miles toward Iwo Jima. The group consisted of the Third, Fourth, and Fifth Divisions of the US Marine Corps.

They departed while the Japanese were distracted by US air attacks on Honshu, Japan's largest island.

The marines hit Iwo Jima's beaches a few days later, landing February 19 through 21. More than 70,000 marines landed on the island that month.[2] The men immediately got to work, battling Japanese troops there. Sometimes, the enemies fought each other in hand-to-hand combat. On the morning of February 23, First Lieutenant Harold Schrier gathered his platoon at the base of Mount Suribachi. There, his boss, Lieutenant Colonel Chandler Johnson, ordered the men to climb the crater, capture it, and raise the US flag.

THE CLIMB

The men charged up the 546-foot (166 m) mountain, moving swiftly in single file. When the landscape steepened, the troops slowed. Being loaded down with arms and ammunition made the march more

CORPS VALUES

The marine corps defines itself by three values: honor, courage, and commitment. Acting honorably includes never cheating, lying, or stealing. It also calls for dedication, dependability, maturity, and trust. Courage is the core of the organization's values. Courage means being strong inside and out, physically, mentally, and morally. Commitment embraces spirit. A Headquarters Marine Corps (HQMC) values statement explains the commitment "leads to professionalism and mastery of the art of war." Commitment affects discipline, dedication, pride, and determination. As HQMC's values statement continues, "Commitment is the value that establishes the Marine as the warrior and citizen others strive to emulate."[3]

IWO JIMA HERO

Jack Lucas, a private first class, was one of the many marines who fought hard to win the Battle of Iwo Jima in 1945. He was young, having turned 17 less than a week before the skirmish. But Lucas was not new to the corps. He had enlisted as a boy of 14, getting in by forging his mother's signature granting permission.

During action, Lucas protected three of his comrades from two grenades. He survived, but with extensive wounds. The grenade explosion lodged more the 250 pieces of shrapnel in his body. Lucas received the Medal of Honor, the US military's highest honor for service personnel, for his brave actions on the tiny island.

challenging. Sometimes the men had to maneuver on their hands and knees. Still, they reached the crater rim in less than 30 minutes.

Schrier halted his men to assess the scene. The marines might be ambushed by Japanese soldiers hiding in the many caves that dotted the landscape. Schrier saw no evidence of the enemy. He ordered his men into the crater to complete their mission.

One by one the men entered the crater. While Schrier had not detected the enemy, the marines proceeded with caution. They spread out and planted themselves near the inside edge of the crater. Half of the group stayed at the crater's edge while the other half headed toward its interior. Suddenly, Japanese soldiers attacked, launching grenades at the marines. The Americans responded with grenades of their own.

While their brothers-in-arms fought the Japanese, Robert Leader and Leo Rozek found some pipe that

Marines fought across the beach with Mount Suribachi looming over them.

appeared to be part of a system to capture rainwater. The piece was long and seemed a good candidate for a flagpole, so the men passed it to those waiting at the summit with the flag: Schrier, Hank Hansen, Chuck Lindberg, and Ernest Thomas. The four men attached the flag to the pole and erected it, planting the metal piece in the ground. The flag fluttered in the wind.

The marines at the base of the mountain saw the stars and stripes whipping in the wind and yelled in celebration, "There goes the flag!"[4] Word of the success spread quickly. Soon, US ships nearby sounded their whistles in support of the achievement.

Japanese troops responded immediately to the raising of the US flag. One man came out of a cave with a rifle. He fired at two Americans and missed. One of them killed the attacker with a flamethrower. Another Japanese fighter charged with a broken sword. Several marines promptly shot him. Next, Japanese soldiers hurled grenades from the caves in which they were hiding. The Americans retaliated with grenades of their own. Then they fired flamethrowers into the entrances and used explosives to blow the caves shut. By this time, more platoons of marines had climbed the mountain. These reinforcements joined in the attack in the crater to capture it from the Japanese.

DO OVER

Approximately three hours after the flag was raised, Johnson decided it should be replaced. The flag had come from the USS *Missoula* and measured 4.5 feet (1.4 m) by 2.3 feet (0.7 m). Seeing their flag flying from Mount Suribachi would bolster US troops' spirits, so Johnson wanted a larger flag raised in place of the one that had been unfurled.

A US amphibious craft beached nearby provided a considerably larger replacement measuring eight feet (2.4 m) by 4.6 feet (1.4 m). Joe Rosenthal, a civilian photographer working for the Associated Press, learned of the replacement flag and headed up Suribachi to record the second raising on film. His photograph quickly gained notice and became an iconic image of the war.

Rosenthal's photograph captured the spirit and courage of the US Marines.

BATTLING ON TO VICTORY

Fighting on the island continued for a few weeks, and the United States declared victory on Iwo Jima on March 26. The win was not without great cost. The battle ended with 26,000 American casualties, 6,800 of them deaths. Only a small fraction of the Japanese who fought survived: 1,083 of 20,000.[5] It was the bloodiest battle of the war and the worst in US Marine Corps history.

The taking of Mount Suribachi brought the United States closer to victory and the war closer to an end. US forces used the island as planned, and by the end of the war, 2,400 bombers transporting 27,000 men had landed

MARINE SLOGANS

Just as companies have slogans for their products or services, so do the branches of the US military. Currently, the marine corps' advertising slogan is "The Few. The Proud. The Marines." This has not always been the corps' advertising tagline. During the Vietnam War, the marine corps was forthright with its "We Don't Promise You a Rose Garden."[8] During the 1980s and 1990s, advertising proclaimed, "We're Looking for a Few Good Men."[9] However, that statement was not new for the branch. William Jones, a captain, advertised in Boston, Massachusetts, on March 20, 1779, for "a few good men" to join the corps' ranks.[10]

on Iwo Jima.[6] The hard work of the marines and the other servicemen who fought helped the United States and its allies win the war in 1945.

THE MEANING OF MOUNT SURIBACHI

For the US Marine Corps, the taking of Mount Suribachi is a highlight in the organization's illustrious history. On that historic day in 1945, James Forrestal, the secretary of the navy, watched the band of dedicated soldiers raise the US flag high on enemy soil. Knowing the importance of the event, he said, "The raising of that flag on Suribachi means a Marine Corps for the next 500 years."[7]

More than once in its history, the marine corps had faced the possibility of being disbanded. Established to fight for the freedom of a yet-to-be nation, the corps began as a water-focused military force. With time, its mission and skills grew, encompassing land and then air. Battle after battle, the military branch proved its worth. And Iwo Jima was no exception. But the victory on Mount Suribachi has meant more.

The iconic photograph Rosenthal snapped that day in February 1945 stands larger than life in the Marine Corps War Memorial. For members past and present, the moment serves as a daily reminder of the sacrifices marines from all generations have made and continue to make to themselves and to their country. They believe wholeheartedly that serving is a privilege.

US MARINE CORPS WAR MEMORIAL

Located in Arlington, Virginia, the US Marine Corps War Memorial is a larger-than-life bronze and granite statue of the raising of the flag on Iwo Jima. The memorial stands almost 80 feet (24 m) tall, with the figures standing 32 feet (10 m) high. The flagpole is 60 feet (18 m) long. The memorial includes a flag that flies constantly. The base reads, "In honor and in memory of the men of the United States Marine Corps who have given their lives to their country since November 10, 1775."[11] Felix W. de Weldon sculpted the piece, basing it on Joe Rosenthal's famous photograph. President Dwight D. Eisenhower dedicated the memorial on November 10, 1954, the corps' one-hundred-seventy-ninth birthday.

CHAPTER TWO
BIRTH OF THE CORPS

When marines captured Mount Suribachi for the United States in February 1945, their branch of the military was well into its second century. The US Marine Corps is as old as the country itself, though it started with a different name: Continental marines.

The Continental marines played a key role in the Revolutionary War, attacking the British in the Bahamas and participating in other battles.

The American Revolution began on April 19, 1775, when British soldiers and colonists in Lexington and Concord, Massachusetts, fought. In May, colonists captured Fort Ticonderoga and Crown Point, located on Lake Champlain in New York. Connecticut and New York provided support by sending marines. These men were more than people who worked in or around water. They were fighters. And their skills at combat and with navigating water made them valuable as defenders of the colonies.

As the colonists continued their battle for independence from Great Britain, the Second Continental Congress deliberated how to proceed. This delegation of representatives from the 13 colonies began meeting in Philadelphia, Pennsylvania, on May 10. They debated a variety of topics, including uniting their colonies'

MARINES: A NATURAL DEVELOPMENT

When marines were called to serve during the American Revolution, many men were skilled on the water for a variety of reasons. England had established its own branch of marines, the Maritime Regiment of Foot, in 1664 to fight the Dutch. When the British established colonies in America, the concept continued in the New World. Many colonists served as marines for the British before the revolution, during the Seven Years' War (1756–1763). These marines excelled in shooting and throwing grenades as well as boarding enemy ships.

Many American colonists lived on the Atlantic Ocean or near rivers and had ample opportunities to gain nautical expertise. During this time, America's waterways were busy with fishing, shipping, and travel. And young men in port cities often joined the crews on merchant ships, where they learned how to work with and climb rigging. They also learned to use the weapons common to such ships, which were armed to fight pirates and privateers.

Privateering was common. The government allowed this piracy on a private scale through letters of marque that granted privateers leeway to seize ships and their cargoes. As a result, the colonies often fought. Together, these factors created a generous pool of men to draw from in creating a band of marine fighters.

respective forces into a single militia to fight the British. Congress formed the Continental army on June 14, 1775.

In August, General George Washington, commander of the new Continental army, sent two schooners to guard the coast of New England. Washington organized marines to man the ships, pulling the men from his army.

Colonial leaders soon realized they would need a water-focused continental force to challenge Great Britain's naval strength. The delegates created the Continental navy on October 13.

In November, the Maritime Committee, headed by John Adams, met at Tun Tavern in Philadelphia. The men drafted the "Rules for the Regulation of the Navy of the United Colonies" and the "Navy Pay List" for the newly established navy.[1] They also wrote a resolution establishing a Continental marines to present to Congress for approval. On November 10, Congress approved the Maritime Committee's resolution and officially created a military branch of marines for the colonies.

The main purpose of members of the newly designated branch would be to serve on ships.

CONTINENTAL PAY

The first men to serve in the Continental marines received pay in the form of money and rations. Each month, a private got six and two-thirds dollars, one pound (0.5 kg) each of bread and beef or pork, one pound of potatoes or turnips or a half pint (0.2 L) of peas, and a half pint of rum. And they sometimes got butter, cheese, and pudding.[2]

There, marines would provide security, protecting officers and crew. They would also act as a floating infantry, able to man guns and board enemy ships.

The first man to head the Continental marines was Samuel Nicholas. He was an innkeeper in Philadelphia.

Engraving of Tun Tavern, which burned down in 1781

Robert Mullan, the owner of Tun Tavern, was named a captain, honored for his ability to recruit marines.

THEIR FIRST EXPEDITION

Within weeks, Nicholas was training a band of 268 marines.[3] Their first assignment would be to take over New Providence, an island in the Bahamas. The British kept a stash of arms and gunpowder there. Washington needed it for his army.

The battalion headed to the island on February 17, 1776, and arrived on March 3. The marines attacked two forts and captured the British governor. The men succeeded in taking a variety of useful items, including dozens of cannons, 15 mortar shells, and thousands of shots. The men found 24 barrels of gunpowder, considerably less than was expected, because the British had moved much of it away.[4] The bounty took two weeks to load and required taking possession of a schooner to help ferry it to the colonies. The attack on New Providence was the Continental marines' first amphibious assault.

END OF THE REVOLUTION: A NEW PHASE FOR THE MARINES

On returning to the colonies, the Continental marines continued fighting for independence from the British. In September 1781, the Continental marines completed their last mission. After the Treaty of Paris ended the

THE FIRST MARINE KILLED

While the booty the Continental marines obtained in New Providence was not as bountiful as hoped, the marines had a successful first expedition. But they encountered trouble on the return trip.

Captain Samuel Nicholas and his marines clashed with the HMS *Glasgow*, a British ship equipped with 20 guns. The Americans suffered casualties. John Fitzpatrick, a second lieutenant, was killed, becoming the first marine officer to lose his life in action. Six other marines died and four were wounded.[6]

war on April 11, 1783, the new US Congress disbanded the Continental navy and marines. Nicholas returned to Philadelphia. In a matter of years, the new government would realize its mistake.

With the United States now independent from the British Empire, its ships were no longer protected by the British navy when trading abroad. In 1796, Congress approved funds to pay for three ships: the *Constellation*, *Constitution*, and *United States*. On April 30, 1798, the US government established the Department of the Navy. President John Adams signed a bill into law on July 11 creating the US Marine Corps.

The branch would be part of the navy. The new corps had 33 officers and 848 noncommissioned officers, musicians, and privates, the last of which was the lowest in rank.[5] Adams named William Ward Burrows major commandant. The US Marine Corps was now official, complete with a leader, hundreds of members, and a name reflecting the

The US Marine Corps was created during John Adams's presidency.

new nation. Its assignment was simple: "any . . . duty on shore as the President, at his discretion, shall direct."[7]

US forces moved in on the Barbary Coast to battle pirates.

CHAPTER THREE
THE 1800s

As the United States moved into a new century and grew into its status as an independent nation, the US Marines grew as well. The 1800s found marines fighting near and far. Before the century was over, they would fight against each other. In the early 1800s, piracy was a

problem for countries attempting to trade and sell goods
in the Mediterranean. Along the Barbary Coast of North
Africa, pirates often attacked merchant ships. The
pirates would take goods and sometimes hold the crews
for ransom.

A FIGHT IN TRIPOLI

For years, the United States paid pirate states such as Morocco and Tunis to protect US merchant ships. In May 1801, Yusuf Caramanli, the leader of Tunis, declared war against the United States when the nation refused to pay enough money in tribute for the protection of US ships in the area. President Thomas Jefferson sent a navy squadron to the Mediterranean to battle pirates. The sailors and marines sent to the Barbary Coast were to protect US merchant ships. The plan was to form a blockade at Tripoli as well.

US forces on the *Enterprise* battled Tripolitan pirates aboard the *Tripoli* in August 1801. The Americans won readily. Marines played an important role. In addition to being skilled musket shooters, these men kept the pirates from boarding the US ship. In the three-hour fight, the Americans killed two-thirds of the *Tripoli*'s crew.

Fighting in the Mediterranean continued for a few years. Then, in 1805, Presley N. O'Bannon, a marine lieutenant, and William Eaton, a general and agent of the US Navy, set out on an ambitious mission: replace Caramanli with his brother, Hamet, who had been in exile in Egypt.

O'Bannon and Eaton led a band of men and camels on a 600-mile (1,000 km) trek across the Libyan Desert to Derna, a city in Tripoli. Numbering 400 men with

O'Bannon and Eaton, the determined group included mercenaries from the Mediterranean, camel drivers, and seven marines.[1] The journey across the desert took more than a month.

In late April, the group started the revolt in the Battle of Derna. The marines led the charge, attacking with a single cannon while three navy ships bombed Tripoli from the harbor. The marines won control of the city's fort, and O'Bannon raised the US flag there, forcing Tripoli to surrender. The war with Tripoli was over.

THE MEXICAN-AMERICAN WAR

In April 1846, the United States began a war with Mexico. The two countries were fighting over Texas, which the United States had annexed the year before. The war lasted until February 1848. The United States emerged victorious, gaining more than 500,000 square miles (1.3 million sq km) of land from Mexico that stretched from the Rio Grande River west to the Pacific Ocean.

THE MAMELUKE

To show his thanks for the marines' help in the Battle of Derna, Hamet gave Lieutenant O'Bannon a Mamluk sword. The Mamluk warrior class ruled Egypt from 1250 to 1517. The Mamluk warriors used this Turkish-style sword. The marine corps made the sword part of the official officer uniform in 1825, referring to it as Mameluke, an alternate spelling. However, officers had already been wearing the sword unofficially. The sword is the oldest ceremonial weapon of all the US military branches.

During the war, American forces invaded Mexico. On March 9, 1847, US Army and US Marine Corps troops landed three miles (5 km) south of Veracruz, on the Gulf of Mexico. General Winfield Scott of the US Army led the 10,000 men in the largest amphibious landing in US history before World War II.[2] By March 29, the Americans had taken the city. From there, they headed west to Mexico City, the capital of Mexico.

The US troops made their way to the Citadel of Chapultepec, a castle overlooking Mexico City. The American force faced 30,000 Mexicans, approximately three times their number.[3] On September 13, the Americans attacked the citadel and took control of the city's entrance, the San Cosme Gate, and then made their way into the city.

The next day, the marines took over the National Palace, which was also known as the Halls of Montezuma in honor of the historic Aztec chief. They removed the Mexican flag and raised the US flag to mark their success. The battles in Tripoli and Mexico are noted in the first line of the "Marines' Hymn": "From the Halls of Montezuma to the shores of Tripoli, we fight our country's battles in the air, on land, and sea."[4]

Landing of US troops at Veracruz

THE AMERICAN CIVIL WAR

Little more than a decade after the war with Mexico, the
American Civil War (1861–1865) divided the United States,
pitting Americans against each other. The marine corps
was divided as well. Marines who had once served united
fought each other as Union marines and Confederate
marines. Before the war, the marine corps had 1,892
members.[5] Many of them resigned to fight for the South.
Half of the marines' captains and two-thirds of their
lieutenants left and joined the Confederate marines.

The Union won, ending the division of the nation.
But the corps' future was uncertain. After the war, the
federal government once again considered disbanding the
corps. With the tumult concluded, there seemed little need

for the military branch. However, Congress determined in 1867 to continue the fighting force: "No good reason appears either for abolishing it, the Marine Corps, or transferring it to the army; on the contrary the Committee recommends that its organization as a separate Corps be preserved and strengthened."[6]

MARINES NEAR AND FAR

Following the war, the US government looked to growing the young nation's status and power in the world, and the corps set to work protecting its country, people, and holdings in places near and far.

The United States grew its navy, sending marines in advance to ready the way for the navy's arrival and to protect developing bases. As part of the US Navy, the US Marine Corps acted as a ground force for its fellow military

MARINE CORPS MOTTOES

The marine corps has had a collection of mottoes over the years. The marines who served during the Revolutionary War followed the words Don't Tread on Me.

Some mottoes have been in Latin, including *Fortitudine*, which means "with courage." During the Mexican-American War, *Per marem, per terram*, or "by sea, by land," emerged. *Semper fidelis*, or "Always faithful," developed after the Civil War. When the US government considered disbanding the corps, navy officers who had served alongside or commanded marines during the war wrote to politicians in support of keeping the military branch. The officers called the military men "Our ever faithful Marines." The words *Semper fidelis* appeared for the first time in the marine corps emblem in 1867. The corps adopted the phrase as its official motto in 1883. Marines often use the short form *Semper fi* as a greeting and a good-bye.[7]

branch. These missions and others took marines around the world. The 30 years following the American Civil War found these men at work in Argentina, Chile, China, Colombia, Egypt, Formosa (present-day Taiwan), Haiti, Hawaii, Japan, Korea, Mexico, Panama, Samoa, and Uruguay.

Richard Harding Davis, a reporter, covered the corps in Panama in 1885. He wrote, "The Marines have landed and have the situation well in hand."[8] As the world headed into a new century, the phrase would continue to ring true.

THE FIRST MEDAL OF HONOR

During the American Civil War, Corporal John F. Mackie became the first marine ever to receive the Medal of Honor, the highest military award in the United States. It is given to one who sets himself apart "by gallantry and [bravery] at the risk of his life above and beyond the call of duty while engaged in an action against an enemy of the United States."[9] Mackie received the award for his actions on the USS *Galena* during the Battle of Drewry's Bluff in Virginia. When Confederate fighters wounded or killed most of his crewmates, Mackie refused to give up. He took over the ship's gun and continued to fight.

T he 1900s brought the marine corps another round of support from the US government. On November 12, 1908, President Theodore Roosevelt solidified the corps' existence with an executive order. In it, he specified the marines would be the country's first line of defense overseas, among other roles.

The US Marines welcomed its first female members in 1918.

The marine corps was growing in support and scale. The 1900s sent the marine corps—and the world—in a new direction. The dawn of aviation put people in the air in motorized vehicles. On August 20, 1912, First Lieutenant Alfred A. Cunningham became the first marine to fly solo. Marine corps aviation was born.

WORLD WAR I: BATTLE OF BELLEAU WOOD

In 1914, war erupted in Europe. The United States sent forces to aid its allies in defeating the Germans beginning in 1917. For the US Marines, one battle stands out: Belleau Wood.

In June 1918, a band of 8,000 marines, as well as hundreds of US Army troops and a few US Navy medical personnel, met and challenged German troops in Belleau Wood, located 30 miles (48 km) outside Paris, France.[1] French troops who had been fighting the Germans ran away and advised the marines to do the same.

But the marines stayed and fought hard for 20 days. Marine sharpshooters hit their targets successfully from hundreds of yards away, which surprised the enemy.

WOMEN MARINES

The marine corps accepted its first female member on August 13, 1918. That day, Opha Mae Johnson enlisted in the Marine Corps Reserve. At the time, women did not go into war areas. They helped behind the scenes, doing clerical work that allowed the men who normally performed it to go into combat. That year, approximately 300 women joined Johnson in serving the corps and their country in this capacity. Their contribution allowed the male marines who normally performed those duties to fight.

In 1948, women were allowed to join the regular corps. On June 12 of that year, the US government made such service possible by passing the Women's Armed Services Integration Act. By the mid-1970s, women marines could work in all areas except aircrew, armor, artillery, and infantry. In 2012, approximately 7 percent of marines were women.[2]

Bombs and gunfire were continuous. Marines dug shallow holes to shield themselves. Both sides suffered major losses. The corps lost more men in that battle alone than during its entire existence to that point.[3] The Americans emerged triumphant, and their success was critical. The marines had kept Paris from the Germans. This gave hope to the Allies—the United States, Great Britain, France, and others—and shook Germany's confidence, helping pave the way for an Allied victory in November 1918.

WORLD WAR II: FOCUSED ON THE PACIFIC

Europe was engulfed in World War II in September 1939 after Germany invaded Poland. Germany was on its way to taking over Europe. For two years, Great Britain and France—the Allies—battled Adolf Hitler and his Nazis, making little progress. The United States became an active participant in the war on December 8, 1941, after Japan, Germany's ally, bombed Pearl Harbor, Hawaii. Americans fought German troops in Europe and Japanese troops in the Pacific.

The corps focused on the Pacific. Of the 485,053 marines who fought in World War II, more than 450,000 of them did so in that part of the world.[4] There, each of the marine corps' amphibious assaults took US forces, including the navy and the army, closer to Japan. Major corps confrontations include Guadalcanal in 1942 and

Tarawa and Cape Gloucester in 1943. In 1944, marines fought on Saipan, Tinian, and Guam in the summer and on Peleliu in the fall. The historic battle for Iwo Jima took place in February and March of 1945. Marines fought the final battle of the Pacific on Okinawa immediately afterward, from April to June.

More than 10,000 marine pilots took to the air above the Pacific Ocean to battle enemy fighter planes. These Americans shot down 2,344 Japanese aircraft.[5] The marine corps flyers provided important support to marines on the ground and strengthened an already strong military branch. The corps had proven itself adept on water, land, and air.

NAVAJO CODE TALKERS

During World War II, both sides used codes to share information while keeping it from the enemy. Cryptographers, or code talkers, were people who encrypt, or encode, messages. They also worked at decoding the enemy's messages.

During the war, the marine corps relied on a little-used language to encode messages: Navajo. Marines from this Native American group used their language as a basis for encrypting messages. Because so few people knew Navajo, the enemy could not break the code.

Not only were Navajo code talkers skilled with their own code, they were quicker and better with codes than any machine. In one test, Navajo code talkers took 20 seconds to encode, send, and decode three lines of English that took machines 30 minutes to do.[6]

The code talkers took part in every marine corps attack in the Pacific from 1942 to 1945, sending messages via radio and telephone. The skills of these marines helped the Allies win the war.

KOREAN WAR: INCHON AND CHOSIN

By 1950, the United States was pulled into another battle in Asia: the Korean War (1950–1953). The United States was helping South Korea fight North Korea.

On September 15, 1950, marines landed at Inchon, behind enemy lines. In the surprise attack on the port city, the men approached by water. Shallow water, shifting sandbars, poor beaches, and the incoming tide made the task challenging. But the marines promptly took the beach and headed inland. Two weeks later, the men took control of the city of Seoul, which was under North Korean occupation.

The successful retaking of Seoul sent the North Koreans running. After landing at Hungnam on the east coast, the marines of the corps' First Division pushed inland. The division was just west of Chosin Reservoir's southern point when they ran into trouble: approximately 100,000 Chinese troops.[7] China had entered the war to aid North Korea.

Five US Army and eight South Korean divisions fled when the Chinese troops arrived, leaving behind weapons, equipment, and the US Marines First Division. It was not a proud moment for the US military.

With 20,000 men, the First was greatly outnumbered by the Chinese.[8] The winter was bitterly cold and frostbite was common. The men made their way dozens of miles back to the sea with their casualties in tow, refusing to leave them behind. Facing the worst weather in decades and greatly outnumbered, the marines in the First suffered severe losses: 4,385 to fighting and 7,338 to the cold. But the Chinese suffered far greater losses: an estimated 40,000 to 80,000 casualties, including losses to the cold.[9]

A US Marine Corps statement says of the event, "No Marines have ever faced worse weather, terrain, or odds than those who fought at Chosin Reservoir, but to anyone familiar with the Marines' spirit of determination, there

MONTFORD POINT

On June 25, 1941, President Franklin D. Roosevelt signed an executive order decreeing "fair employment by the armed forces," opening the armed services to nonwhites.[10] The African-American men who enlisted in the marine corps trained at a segregated facility: Montford Point, part of Camp Lejeune in North Carolina.

Gene Doughty was one of Montford's first recruits. He said of the segregation, "We felt it was an indignity that was thrown at us, but we had to learn and had to face all these challenges we had." Doughty was assigned to the segregated Thirty-Sixth Depot Company. He served on Iwo Jima and was part of the Normandy invasion in June 1944. Robert D. Reld trained at Montford in 1948. He shared, "My drill instructor . . . told us that if you are going to be a black Marine, you are going to have to be better than anyone else."[11] It was the beginning of his 26-year career in the corps.

In July 1948, President Harry S. Truman ordered that military segregation end. The marine corps stopped training at Montford in September 1949 and trained recruits in integrated units from then on. From 1942 to 1949, the corps trained approximately 20,000 African-American recruits at Montford.[12]

The cold, snowy conditions at Chosin complicated the marines' mission.

was no doubt the First Marine Division would prevail."[13] While the war ended in a stalemate, the US Marine Corps once again proved itself as a reliable, skilled, and determined fighting force.

VIETNAM WAR: OPERATION SHUFLY

The 1960s found the United States at war in Asia again. The Vietnam War dragged on for more than two decades, lasting from 1954 to 1975. The US Marines helped South Vietnam during the war. Marines provided the amphibious and ground fighting for which the branch had become known. The corps also showed its skill in the air.

One key corps mission was Operation Shufly, which called on helicopter squadrons to aid ground troops. It was the first air support marine unit deployed to Vietnam. Marine Task Unit 79.3.5 landed on April 15, 1962. The operation lasted until March 8, 1965. Throughout, the marine corps gained valuable experience in moving troops with helicopters.

Lieutenant Colonel Archie Clapp led the first squadron to serve in the mission. The group included 24 UH-34 Seahorse helicopters, to which the commanding general added three OE-1 Birddog fixed-wing Cessna airplanes, a C-117 Skytrain, and 50 helicopter mechanics. The Cessna was for gathering information. The Skytrain would move men and supplies.

The marines learned important lessons from fighting in Vietnam. One was not to send out a helicopter alone. Clapp understood the danger of being shot down. He said, "I had enough of that feeling of flying over enemy territory where you might be shot down and captured right away. I wouldn't have that happen with my people. So they went in pairs, and nobody had done that before."[14]

The mission started another practice. The helicopters of Operation Shufly were at the ready in the air near ground battles, with troops aboard. The helicopters could

Marines changed the way helicopters were used
in combat during the Vietnam War.

drop in where needed and unload troops to support the
men already fighting.

Another advance was adding running boards to
helicopters. The boards helped fighters get in and out
of a helicopter more easily when speed was critical.
Marine helicopter squadrons today still employ practices
established during Operation Shufly.

Operation Shufly was a buildup to major US
involvement in Vietnam. In July 1965, President Lyndon
Johnson approved deployment of 100,000 troops to the

Asian nation, followed by another 100,000 the next year.[15] US participation continued growing, but the war proved unwinnable. By 1973, when the United States began withdrawing its troops, the corps alone had suffered more than 100,000 casualties, almost 13,000 of them deaths.[16]

DESERT STORM: STORMING KUWAIT

On August 2, 1990, Iraq invaded Kuwait. Saddam Hussein, Iraq's leader, wanted to expand his power in the area and take control of Kuwait's expansive reserves of oil.

When the United Nations ordered Iraq to leave Kuwait on August 3, Hussein refused. On August 8, Iraq officially annexed its small neighbor. The United States, its allies in Western Europe, Egypt, and other countries of the Middle East joined forces to fight Iraq, which had approximately 300,000 troops in Kuwait. If Iraq did not withdraw by

THE BOMBING IN BEIRUT

In the early 1980s, the United States stationed service members in Beirut, Lebanon, as part of a peacekeeping force. France, Italy, and the United Kingdom also sent troops. Lebanon was in the middle of a civil war. For a time after US servicemen arrived in August 1982, the situation seemed to be going well. But on April 18, 1983, terrorists struck the US embassy in West Beirut with a car bomb. The attack killed dozens of Americans and Lebanese.

Fighting between local military groups and the peacekeeping forces grew over the following months. Then, on October 23, 1983, suicide bombers attacked two locations. One was a US Marine Corps barracks. The other was housing for French paratroopers. The French lost 58 soldiers. Of the 241 Americans killed, 220 were Marines. For the corps, it was the highest single-day loss of life since the battle for Iwo Jima almost 40 years earlier.[17]

At Camp Pendleton, California, marines trained for desert conditions in preparation for a mission in Iraq.

January 15, 1991, the United States and its allies would strike. By January, the number of anti-Iraq coalition troops was 700,000. Of these, 540,000 were US military members.[18]

On January 16, the coalition forces began attacking Iraq as part of Operation Desert Storm. Their extensive air strikes lasted for weeks. Marine pilots helped demolish a variety of Iraqi locations and equipment. Meanwhile, ground forces went to work, attacking from the north and the south. These marines met many dangers, including artillery attacks, barbed wire, booby traps, and flaming trenches. Visibility was limited because oil fields burned, creating heavy, dark smoke that made day as dark as night.

On February 25, marines crossed from Saudi Arabia into Kuwait. One battalion of marine corps tanks fought Iraqis for three and one-half hours. By the end of the exchange, the Americans emerged victorious, demolishing 25 armored vehicles and 50 tanks and taking more than 300 prisoners.[19] The war ended within days of the marines taking Kuwait.

The 1900s found marines in battles across the globe. Adding to its amphibious skills, the corps proved itself in ground combat and in the air. Today, this expertise makes the corps valuable in its role as the United States' go-to ground combat force and for a variety of other missions, including providing humanitarian aid.

MARINE CASUALTIES IN WARS[20]

War/Battle	Killed	Wounded	Total
American Revolutionary War (April 19, 1775– April 11, 1783)	49	70	119
War of 1812 (June 18, 1812– February 17, 1815)	45	66	111
Mexican-American War (April 24, 1846– May 30, 1848)	11	47	58
American Civil War (Union forces only) (April 15, 1861– May 26, 1865)	148	131	279
Spanish-American War (February 15, 1898– December 10, 1898)	6	21	27
World War 1 (April 6, 1917– November 11, 1918)	2,461	9,520	11,981
World War II (December 7, 1941– December 31, 1946)	19,733	68,207	87,940
Korean War (June 25, 1950– January 31, 1955)	4,267	23,744	28,011
Vietnam War (August 4, 1964– January 27, 1973)	13,095	88,594	101,689
Gulf War (August 2, 1990– March 3, 1991)	24	92	116
Operation Enduring Freedom, Afghanistan (October 7, 2001– March 20, 2014)[21]	453	4,915	5,368
Operation Iraqi Freedom, Iraq (March 19, 2003– March 20, 2014)[22]	1,023	8,626	9,649

CHAPTER FIVE
THE MARINE CORPS' MISSIONS

The US Marine Corps is an expeditionary force, known for its immediate response in times of strife. Marines are trained and prepared to deploy at a moment's notice to help those in need, whether in times of combat or after disaster strikes.

Marines form a convoy on December 13, 2001, in preparation for an attack on Kandahar, Afghanistan.

Following the terrorist attacks of September 11, 2001, marines and other US military forces focused on fighting al-Qaeda and the Taliban. Marines deployed to Afghanistan in 2001 as part of Operation Enduring Freedom. Marine pilots in F/A-18 Hornet fighter jets started air attacks on October 18. The Marine Corps provided the first major ground troops, supplying 9,000.[1]

The marines fought hard. They captured Kandahar Airport in December 2001 for use as a command center. In February 2002, the Marine Corps handed over control of the base to the US Army, which would use it for long-term operations. These marines had fulfilled their duty of being "first in," going where needed, meeting their objective, and then moving on to their next mission.[2]

In 2003, marines went to Iraq as part of Operation Iraqi Freedom. They fought insurgents, provided security, and helped those in need. They did so for several years, all while continuing to fight as needed in Afghanistan.

SAVING HISTORY IN IRAQ

Matthew Bogdanos was a reservist when the attacks of September 11, 2001, occurred. He was called to active duty and became one of the thousands of marines who served in Iraq. The corps promptly put his master's degree in classical studies to use.

In 2003, looters stole approximately 10,000 items from the National Museum of Iraq in Baghdad, including valuable treasures from the world's earliest civilizations. Bogdanos was tasked with forming a team to find and recover the priceless artifacts. The colonel's strategy was to use the Iraqi people. His team built trust with civilians who then became informants. The plan helped Bogdanos's group recover more than 5,500 of the relics.[3] In the process, the marines created goodwill among Iraqis with whom they worked and discovered a relationship between the world of illegal art dealing and terrorism.

Bogdanos received a medal for his work in Iraq. He also wrote a book about it and gives money he earns from the book to Iraq's National Museum.

In early 2010, marines led Operation Moshtarak in southern Afghanistan. It was the biggest operation since the war began. Marines succeeded at retaking cities from Taliban control. Though a victory for US forces, the mission did not end the fighting in the country. In June 2010, the war in Afghanistan became the longest in US history. The operation in Iraq officially ended in September, replaced with a new mission. Operation New Dawn aimed at helping Iraqis rebuild their war-torn nation.

ALWAYS READY

Swift deployment is the marine corps' forte. As the part of the US military usually sent first into ground combat, the corps is structured to do so at a moment's notice.

Marine expeditionary units (MEUs) make such deployment possible. The MEU is a "self-contained, forward-deployed response force."[4] Marines in MEUs are ready to be called at any time. Usually, an MEU has a variety of vehicles, including helicopters, tanks, jets, bulldozers, dump trucks, forklifts, water purification units, and high-mobility multipurpose wheeled vehicles (HMMWV), otherwise known as Humvees. MEUs can organize and start a mission in less than six hours. The corps can adjust MEUs as needed to meet the needs of a particular mission. MEUs are usually located in or near a

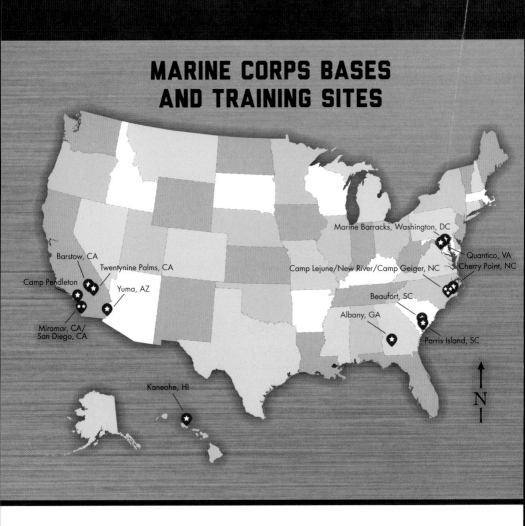

MARINE CORPS BASES AND TRAINING SITES

Marine Barracks, Washington, DC

Barstow, CA

Twentynine Palms, CA

Quantico, VA

Cherry Point, NC

Camp Lejune/New River/Camp Geiger, NC

Camp Pendleton

Yuma, AZ

Beaufort, SC

Miramar, CA/
San Diego, CA

Albany, GA

Parris Island, SC

Kaneohe, HI

N

few locations: the Mediterranean Sea, the Indian Ocean, Northeast Asia, and Southwest Asia.

Today, the branch's combat operations include amphibious raid and assault, antipiracy work, reconnaissance and surveillance, and recovering hostages or aircraft and personnel. In addition to conducting such work when called, the Marine Corps has ongoing projects worldwide. In South America, Marines train those fighting drug organizations in marksmanship and leadership. Marines provide similar training in Africa, helping Nigerians to fight terrorism. In Europe, the headquarters of corps operations on the continent are in Germany. Work in the Pacific and Oceania includes martial arts training in Mongolia, flight training in Thailand, and joint security information and planning sessions for the Pacific with Australia, Canada, and the United Kingdom.

HELPING THOSE IN NEED

Marines also do humanitarian work at home and abroad. The preparedness of its MEUs keeps the marine corps ready to respond when natural disasters or other sudden catastrophes occur.

STATIONED NEAR AND FAR

The corps has 13 bases. They are primarily in the United States, on the East and West Coasts, with two locations in the Pacific. Eastern US locations are in Georgia, North Carolina, South Carolina, and Washington, DC. Western locations are in Southern California and Arizona. The Pacific locations are in Hawaii and Japan. These 13 locations serve as both home and work for thousands of marines stationed at them.

Marine training occurs in five locations. Recruits train at either Marine Corps Recruit Depot San Diego, in California, or Parris Island, in South Carolina. Marines complete additional training at Marine Corps Base Camp Pendleton, in California; Quantico, in Virginia; and Camp Geiger, in North Carolina.

The marine corps' presence extends well beyond its recruit depots, bases, and other locations. Through deployments for combat and humanitarian projects, embassy work, and training, members spend time in a variety of locales. Marines serve on every continent but Antarctica.

TOYS FOR TOTS

Each year, Americans donate toys to Toys for Tots to distribute to children in need. The program began in 1947, when Bill Hendricks, a major in the Marine Corps Reserve, began collecting toys in Los Angeles, California. People donated 5,000 toys that year. In 1948, the marine corps took on and grew Toys for Tots into a national program. Walt Disney designed its train logo.

The Marine Corps Toys for Tots Foundation formed as a nonprofit organization in 1991 to oversee Toys for Tots. The foundation also runs the Toys for Tots Literacy Program, which provides resources to improve the education of economically disadvantaged children.

Toys for Tots succeeds through the generosity of others. The literacy facet of Toys for Tots has received more than $2 million in support of its mission. As of its 2012 toy drive, people had donated almost 17 million toys.[5]

In 2005, Hurricane Katrina hit the Gulf Coast of the United States. The hurricane was the deadliest since 1928. Louisiana and Mississippi suffered terrible flooding. Marines searched for survivors and then helped clean up the damage and rebuild.

In November 2013, marines aided people in the Philippines. The island nation was recovering from Typhoon Haiyan, one of the strongest tropical storms ever recorded to make landfall. People were without clean water. Homes and businesses had been flattened. Marines brought a variety of equipment, including dump trucks, generators, and portable water tanks. By the end of November, Marines had helped more than 8,000 people—mostly Filipinos whose homes had been destroyed—by flying them to other locations. During that

time, the US Marines also transported 1,168 short tons (1,060 metric tons) of relief goods.[6]

A SENSE OF SECURITY

Marines are known as the "First to Fight."[7] The branch's skill, ability, and readiness for combat give many Americans a feeling that is immeasurable: a sense of security. By fighting terrorists firsthand or training others how to do so, the marine corps helps make the world a safer place. As the nation's expeditionary force, the corps is unlike any other military force. General James F. Amos, commander of the marine corps, explained,

> *Because our nation cannot afford to hold the entire joint force at such a high state of readiness, it has chosen to keep the Marines ready, and has often used them to plug the gaps during international crises, to respond when no other options were available. Like an affordable insurance policy, Marine Corps forces represent a very efficient and effective hedge against the nation's most likely risks.*[8]

Regardless of the task, the marine corps is available when and where needed. It is a band of members skilled because of the rigorous training the corps provides.

"Some people spend an entire lifetime wondering if they made a difference in the world. Marines don't have that problem."[9]
—*Ronald Reagan, US president, 1981–1989*

Sea and air vehicles help the marines deploy quickly.

CHAPTER SIX
GETTING THE JOB DONE

As an organization more than 200 years old, the marine corps has changed over the years. The corps of the 2000s honors its history while embracing the present, including the latest technology in weapons, vehicles, aircraft, and gear.

A marine practices firing a javelin missile, one of many advanced marine corps weapons.

The marine corps is structured to allow the best response when called into action. The marine corps is part of the Department of the Navy, along with the US Navy. The corps is divided into three groups. Headquarters, Marine Corps (HQMC) is the first group. HQMC oversees the maintenance of the marines. It is the administrative side of the branch. HQMC's varied tasks affect all marines and include recruiting, training, supplying, and moving them. HQMC also focuses on efficiency and monitors its readiness to aid military operations.

Marine Corps Operating Forces is the next group. It includes Marine Corps Forces, Marine Corps Reserve, Security Forces, and Special Activity Forces. Marine Corps Forces consists of every aviation, combat logistics, and ground unit—the general-purpose fighting units. Marine Corps Reserve includes reservists, the marines who lead civilian lives and serve only when called to duty. Security Forces focuses on antiterrorism and security. These marines protect US locations, ships, and more. Special Activity Forces includes marines posted at embassies and other places abroad.

The third group is the Supporting Establishment, which encompasses all marine corps air stations, bases, and installations. This group supports training, equipping, and transporting marines. That is, it aids HQMC.

In addition to this structure, in combat, the corps organizes its marines in units of varying sizes. From the fire team of four to the army of approximately 250,000, this structure helps the branch respond to missions of any size.[1]

US DEPARTMENT OF DEFENSE BUDGET
FISCAL YEAR 2014[2]

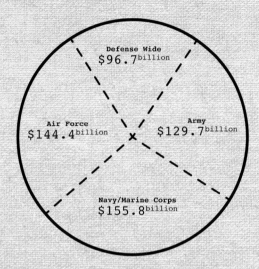

Defense Wide
$96.7 billion

Air Force
$144.4 billion

Army
$129.7 billion

Navy/Marine Corps
$155.8 billion

US MARINE CORPS BUDGET
(OUT OF THE NAVY/MARINE CORPS BUDGET)[3]

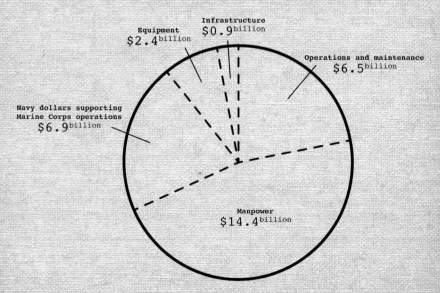

Equipment
$2.4 billion

Infrastructure
$0.9 billion

Operations and maintenance
$6.5 billion

Navy dollars supporting
Marine Corps operations
$6.9 billion

Manpower
$14.4 billion

WEAPONS

Marines have a reputation for being skilled marksmen, trained at using a variety of weapons. These include the M4 Carbine and M16 rifles and the M249 Squad Automatic Weapon. The M9 Beretta is a pistol. And the M240B is a machine gun. Bigger weapons include the M777 howitzer artillery piece, the M110 semiautomatic sniper system, the Browning .50 caliber machine gun, the FGM-148 Javelin antitank missile, and 60mm and 81mm mortars.

Marines fire a M777 howitzer.

Marines also use a bayonet. This knife has a serrated edge and sharp point. A marine can wield the knife by hand or attach it to a rifle.

Grenades are small explosives that can injure and kill. Marines launch them by hand. They also use the M32 and MK19 to launch grenades. The M32 can send out six grenades in less than three seconds. The MK19 can be used with a tripod or on a vehicle, and its fire can destroy a vehicle with armor up to two inches (5 cm) thick.

GEAR

Marines carry carefully selected gear to help them succeed in their missions. Marines are skilled shooters who must shoot accurately at 200, 300, and 500 yards (183, 274, and 457 m). The Rifle Combat Optic (RCO) improves their skills. The RCO is a scope for use with the M4 and the M16A4 rifles. Using the RCO allows marines to hit targets as far away as 875 yards (800 m).

The AN/PEQ-15 and AN/PEQ-16A are rifle optics designed for use with several guns: M4s, M16s, M240Bs, and M249s. The PEQ-15 provides laser targeting, while the PEQ-16 adds light. Using these items comes with a risk: the enemy may see the light and locate marines for attack.

The AN/PVS-14 is a single-eye instrument used to see at night. Marines can hold the device or attach it to their helmet or rifle. Pairing the AN/PVS-14 with the

AN/PEQ-15 and the AN/PEQ-16A further improves a shooter's accuracy.

Combat is not quiet. To protect their hearing, marines wear ballistic hearing protection (BHP). These earplugs are two-sided. One side guards against consistent, loud noises. The other side protects against bursts of sound but allows the wearer to hear general background sounds.

To protect their torsos, marines wear the Improved Modular Tactical Vest (IMTV). The vest protects its wearer against shrapnel and 9mm bullets from a pistol. The IMTV is designed to be as comfortable as possible.

Marines also carry a collection of pouches. They are lightweight and hold equipment such as flares, grenades, magazines, and shotgun shells. There is even a pouch for empty magazines. Marines also carry an individual first aid kit when in combat.

Communication is critical for success and survival. Infantry squads and fire teams rely on

INDIVIDUAL FIRST AID KIT

Marines go into combat carrying an individual first aid kit. The kit is a heavy-duty fabric pouch with a strap, containing a variety of items intended to treat minor injuries. Supplies include a tourniquet; gauze and tape; bandages of different sizes and shapes, some of them adhesive; antibiotic ointment; iodine; and water purification tablets.

First aid training includes viewing images of injuries, watching an instructor use the first aid supplies in demonstrations, and then applying first aid themselves, under the attentive eyes of drill instructors.

the Motorola PRC-153 Integrated Intra-Squad Radio to communicate wirelessly. Marines can use these radios in environments ranging from forests to cities.

VEHICLES

The marine corps has a collection of ground vehicles that navigate all types of terrain, from rugged hills to sandy beaches. The vehicles are designed for a range of purposes.

The MTVR is a large truck great for carrying people and supplies. The corps also uses the vehicle to move the M777 Howitzer.

As a force that works on water and land, the marine corps relies on the AAV-7, an amphibious assault vehicle. This craft carries marines from ships to shore.

MARPAT

In combat, marines wear camouflage to blend in with their surroundings. It has changed throughout the years. The standard pattern of green and shades of brown was for use in woodland areas, while other patterns of tan and brown were for desert wear.

In 2002, the marine corps released a new combat utility uniform with a pattern created by a computer. The pixel design has overlapping squares. MARPAT, short for marine pattern, comes in two versions: woodland and desert. MARPAT is unique, designed to keep both humans and machines from noticing the wearer.

MARPAT uniforms are more durable than the old uniforms. They have pockets on the shoulders and chest pockets with Velcro. They also have a coating to protect wearers from insect bites that might transmit disease.

Initially, only the corps used MARPAT. Eventually, other branches of the US military adopted the uniform.

Marines use a variety of vehicles for shore landings, including inflatable boats.

Marines also use tanks. The M1A1 Abrams tank is the corps' go-to tank. While in battle, marines rely on the Abrams for protection and firepower. The LAV-25, a light armored vehicle, offers speed, maneuverability, and firepower. The craft is also amphibious. Marines use the LAV-25 for several tasks, including assault, combat command, communications transport, and reconnaissance. It also serves as a weapons platform.

Marines use the Humvee in all parts of battle. Marines prefer the mine-resistant ambush-protected all-terrain vehicle (MATV) for off-road work. It performs well in areas with mountains. Marines use both vehicles for ambulance, combat command, and transportation for shelters, troops, and weapons.

For superior big-gun power, marines call on the high-mobility artillery rocket system (HIMARS). The HIMARS is the branch's best artillery system. It has extensive firepower and is able to shoot numerous missiles and rockets as far as 40 miles (64 km), striking within 26 feet (8 m) of the target.

The newest vehicle in the marine corps' arsenal of combat craft is the assault breacher vehicle (ABV). The ABV began its work clearing away mines in Afghanistan in December 2009. This specialized vehicle has a plow for clearing mines, a machine gun, and equipment capable of sending explosives as far as 150 yards (137 m).

AIRCRAFT

In 2012, the corps celebrated 100 years of aviation. The mission of these units is to support ground forces.

The marine corps has a varied collection of aircraft. Jets include the F/A-18 Hornet and AV-8B Harrier II. Helicopters include the AH-1Z Super Cobra/Viper, CH-53E Super Stallion, and UH-1Y Huey/Venom.

The MV-22B Osprey can refuel midair, increasing its range.

The MV-22 Osprey is a combination of an airplane and a helicopter. The aircraft takes off vertically, like a helicopter, and then flies like an airplane. This blend gives it greater speed and broader range than helicopters and more maneuverability than an airplane. The craft can transport 24 marines.

A massive airplane, the KC-130J Super Hercules lives up to its name. The craft is designed to move marines and their supplies, including fuel. The KC-130J is 90 feet (27 m) long. Its wings span 130 feet (40 m). The plane can haul more than 12,000 gallons (45,000 L) of fuel and refuel two aircraft at the same time at 300 gallons (1,100 L) per minute. An armed version of the aircraft can launch air-to-ground missiles, guided bombs, and cannon rounds.

Not all aircraft are manned. The relatively small RQ-7B Shadow is a drone. The RQ-7B is 11.2 feet (3.4 m) long and has a wingspan of 14 feet (4.3 m). The craft aids marines with communications, reconnaissance, and targeting.

Its weapons, gear, vehicles, and aircraft help the marine corps complete tasks worldwide. But these tools are nothing without the skills and practice to use them. Recruits complete rigorous training that makes them worthy of the title *marine*, but only after qualifying for service.

MARINE ONE

The marine corps serves the president of the United States by ferrying the commander in chief in *Marine One*, a VH-3D Sea King helicopter. The craft takes the president short distances, to places near Washington, DC. Sometimes it takes other passengers, airlifting them to points in the United States and beyond. Marines serving the president this way are part of HMX-1, a helicopter squadron based 35 miles (56 km) from the nation's capital at the Quantico marine base. Their duty is considered highly important.

In 2008, the helicopter got its first female pilot: Jennifer Grieves. The major held the position until July 2009, a little longer than the usual period of one year.

CHAPTER SEVEN
BECOMING A MARINE

N ot everyone can become a marine. Joining requires
a recruit to meet multiple eligibility requirements. A
marine is either an officer or an enlisted member. Officers
are similar to managers, while the enlisted are the workers
the officers oversee. In addition, officers tend to operate or
oversee aircraft and ships. Enlisted marines are the

Marines participate in endurance courses throughout their careers to improve their readiness and group spirit.

hands-on people who take part in combat and other missions. They also operate equipment and keep it running properly. Most marines are enlisted. In 2010, there were 204,153 marines: 21,208 officers and 182,945 enlisted.[1] Officers and enlisted marines have different eligibility and training requirements. There are paths for enlisted marines to become officers, too.

OFFICER ELIGIBILITY AND TRAINING

Officer recruits are 20 to 27 years old, US citizens, and have a bachelor's degree in addition to a high school diploma. Officers usually choose one of two routes to becoming an officer. They take the Platoon Leaders Class (PLC) in the summer while in college or they complete the Officer Candidate Course after finishing college. Most marines who become officers do so through the PLC.

Marine officer training takes place at the US Marine Corps' Officer Candidates School (OCS), located in Quantico, Virginia. OCS training includes passing the Physical Fitness Test (PFT) required of all marines throughout their years of service and the Combat Fitness Test (CFT). The test includes a timed run that measures endurance, an ammunition lift that tests strength, and an obstacle course that involves running, crawling, carrying, resupplying ammunition, and throwing grenades.

Another path to becoming an officer is to attend and graduate from the US Naval Academy. There, students live a military life while obtaining an undergraduate degree.

Once they have completed OCS training or graduated from the US Naval Academy, officers study at the Basic

School (TBS). It is also located in Quantico. There, the corps explains, they learn "how to lead and inspire fellow Marines."[2]

Finally, each officer is assigned a military occupational specialty (MOS). The MOS is determined by three factors: the marine corps' needs, the officer's performance, and the officer's preference. The officer will be trained in his or her MOS.

ENLISTED ELIGIBILITY

A person seeking to be enlisted must be 17 to 28 years old at the time of enlistment, a legal resident of the United States, and a high school graduate. In addition to meeting eligibility requirements, potential marines must take two tests.

DELAYED ENTRY PROGRAM

Those who enlist in the marine corps need not begin training immediately. Through the Delayed Entry Program (DEP), a young man or woman interested in joining the corps may put off entering for a period of up to one year after signing the contract to enlist. Delaying entry gives the potential recruit time to investigate, consider, and decide if joining the branch is the right thing to do. During this time, the recruit will have contact with the military branch and begin to develop a feeling of camaraderie with the corps even before officially beginning training. A recruiter will teach the recruit about the corps and also arrange for the recruit to participate in activities related to the corps, such as training events and family nights.

Those who enlist in the marine corps are not called marines until they complete recruit training. The corps refers to aspiring marines taking part in the DEP as "Poolees."[3]

PHYSICAL FITNESS TEST

Once they become recruits, males and females must meet more stringent physical requirements. Every recruit must pass the PFT each year. All marines—officers, too—take the test yearly during their time of active duty to determine their level of physical fitness.

The PFT consists of the same trials as the IST. For the timed run, however, the distance doubles to 3 miles (4.8 km). Males have 28 minutes to complete the task. Females have 31 minutes.

The first test is the Armed Services Vocational Aptitude Battery (ASVAB), also taken by recruits to other branches of the military. The multiple-choice test has questions in several areas related to science, math, literacy, electronics, mechanics, and assembling objects. Testing so many topics helps determine individual abilities the corps can develop. The marine corps uses test scores to assign its members to MOSs.

Potential recruits must also pass the Initial Strength Test (IST). The IST tests physical ability, and the marine corps encourages aspiring marines to be able to exceed its basic standards when they arrive for training. The IST includes running, crunches, and either pull-ups (for males) or a flexed-arm hang (for females), which looks like the top part of a pull-up.

ENLISTED TRAINING

Training to become a marine begins with 12 weeks of boot camp at Parris Island, South Carolina, or San Diego,

Recruits must complete an obstacle course during training at Parris Island in South Carolina.

California. The 12 weeks will test a recruit physically, mentally, and emotionally.

During boot camp, recruits acquire a variety of knowledge and skills. They learn the corps' history, rules, and protocols, as well as military law.

The young men and women go through rigorous physical training to prepare them to be elite fighters. They learn to use a bayonet and a pugil stick. Recruits also learn to shoot a variety of guns. They practice shooting an M16 standing, kneeling, sitting, and lying flat on the ground. Recruits learn hand-to-hand combat in the Marine Corps Martial Arts Program (MCMAP).

Recruits learn to rappel, too. Learning this skill builds confidence and courage. They also learn hand signals and how to move under barbed wire and over walls. Teamwork is another important skill.

"We believe that Marines are forged in a furnace of shared hardship and tough training. This common, intense experience creates bonds of comradeship and standards of conduct so strong that Marines will die for each other. This belief will continue to be the basis upon which we make Marines."[4]
—US Marine Corps Recruit Training Manual

The last phase of training, called the crucible, challenges recruits physically and mentally. For 54 hours straight, with little food or sleep, a recruit faces challenges alone and as part of a team. Completing this final test earns a recruit the distinction of marine.

The marine corps does more than teach recruits history and provide physical and weapons training. The corps breaks down recruits and then builds them back up. In their 12 weeks at boot camp, recruits become confident in their ability to fight. But their confidence is greater than simply knowing they can go into combat as physically prepared as possible. Marines know they can rely on each other to fight to the death.

For those who pass boot camp, the marine corps honors their success in the Emblem Ceremony. During the event, drill instructors give each recruit in their platoon the eagle, globe, and anchor—a pin of the marine corps emblem. Instructors also call their recruits "marine" for the first time.

After two weeks of vacation, recruits return to duty for advanced training focused on an MOS. Depending on the MOS, a marine might train for more than a year to learn his or her specialty.

THE PLEDGE

Every recruit takes a pledge when joining the marine corps, vowing to devote himself or herself to the US Constitution:

I, [Name], do solemnly swear (or affirm) that I will support and defend the Constitution of the United States against all enemies, foreign and domestic; that I will bear true faith and allegiance to the same; and that I will obey the orders of the President of the United States and the orders of the officers appointed over me, according to the regulations and the Uniform Code of Military Justice. So help me God.[5]

A DAY AT THE NAVAL ACADEMY

As part of the US Navy, the marine corps' college is the US Naval Academy, located in Annapolis, Maryland. Students graduate with a bachelor of science degree in one of 25 majors. They may participate in extracurricular activities. More than 70 are available, including heritage clubs, music, theater, religious groups, and sports.

As a military institution, the academy teaches students military life. This includes a very structured schedule that covers every part of the day, from reveille at 6:30 a.m. through lights out at midnight. Meals are at 7:15 a.m., 12:10 p.m., and from 6:30 p.m. to 7:15 p.m. Morning classes—four of them at 50 minutes each—are between 7:55 a.m. and 11:45 a.m. Two more classes are held after lunch, between 1:30 p.m. and 3:30 p.m.

In the afternoon, from 3:45 p.m. to 6:00 p.m., students may take part in school sports, extracurricular activities, and personal business. In the fall and spring, drill and parades take place twice each week. Finally, 8:00 p.m. to 11:00 p.m. is study time.

In addition to all of these activities, students also must meet military duties, including inspections. And sometimes, a student may have additional studies. Demands are many.

New officers in the navy, *in white*, and marine corps, *in blue*, traditionally toss their hats into the air upon graduating from the US Naval Academy.

CHAPTER EIGHT

CAREER OPPORTUNITIES

Every marine is trained for combat, particularly in how to use guns. "Every Marine a Rifleman" is a corps creed.[1] The marine corps also provides training to perform specific roles. The skills learned in each MOS prepare a marine for work in the branch. MOSs are designed to make the marine corps the best it can be. The roles are varied

and numerous. The 450 MOSs are classified in more than 40 categories, most of which fall into one of four groups: ground combat, aviation combat, logistics combat, and command.[2]

US MARINE SECURITY GUARDS

US Marine Security Guards (MSGs) serve at US embassies and consulates in 137 countries.[3] MSGs are stationed at embassy entrances, but they do more than stand guard. These marines protect citizens, property, and government information of the United States in various situations, including attack, such as the bombing of the US embassy in Beirut, Lebanon, in 1983.

Training includes being doused with pepper spray, learning about weapons, and engaging in one-on-one defensive maneuvers. MSGs must also obtain a high-level security clearance, a special approval from the government. Once they complete MSG training, these marines complete three years of MSG duty at an embassy.

GROUND COMBAT ELEMENT

The ground combat element (GCE) is the core of the corps. Most marines are part of GCE, which includes infantry, field artillery, amphibious assault, reconnaissance, and tank and engineer forces. Each of these areas has specific MOSs. For example, an enlisted marine in the infantry might be a rifleman, a machine gunner, a mortarman, or an assaultman. The marine in each of these roles will have completed initial training in the Infantry Training Battalion course and then studied his or her specialty.

Officers also serve in the infantry. They train the enlisted infantry in different combat situations and in all environments. These officers also collect and analyze information about the enemy, create plans for fighting, and oversee their group's equipment and weapons use.

AVIATION COMBAT ELEMENT

When the marines are needed in the air, the aviation combat element goes to work. Officers in this element fly the aircraft, while enlisted personnel keep the aircraft going.

Jobs available are numerous. Enlisted members of an aircrew might work as aerial observers/gunners, who use a machine gun in combat in the air and also maintain

Some marines specialize in helicopter maintenance.

the aircraft. A helicopter crew chief specializes in aircraft maintenance. Other specialties include air traffic control, aircraft maintenance and repair, aviation electronics, aviation intelligence, aviation operations, aircrew membership, meteorology, and weapon system support.

An officer might be a pilot or an air traffic control officer. Aviation maintenance officers oversee the enlisted air maintenance personnel and keep maintenance on track. Officers in this MOS also schedule aircraft inspections and manage supplies and equipment.

LOGISTICS COMBAT ELEMENT

Combat logistics is critical to the smooth operation of a variety of elements, from people to supplies to equipment. The roles a marine can choose in combat logistics are broad. Jobs available, depending on the marine's rank,

DOG HANDLER

Dogs also play a role in the marine corps, particularly in detecting bombs. Over the course of six weeks, a dog and a marine specializing in dog handling develop a bond through many hours of training. During that time, the dog learns how to detect bombs and how to bite in a way that ends a difficult situation, and the handler learns to help a dog do these things.

The bond between dog and handler is important to their success as military members. The relationship between the two develops through more than training. The handler plays with, feeds, and walks the dog. Once the two establish a bond through these everyday activities, they focus on bomb detection and bite work. Sergeant Joshua Sutherland is a dog handler. He said of his job, "It's great getting to work with dogs every day. No day is the same, and not many people get to do my job."[4]

Marines form deep bonds with their dog partners.

include engineering, construction, transportation, personnel and administration, supply, communications, and equipment and vehicle repair.

In the area of communications, an enlisted marine might become a field operator and be responsible for setting up and operating all the radio equipment in a mission. Communications specialists make it possible for ground forces to communicate during a mission. Another option is data network specialist. This marine works with communications from the computer side, setting up and maintaining a computer network.

Officers in the logistics combat element take on a range of roles similar to the enlisted marines. For example, adjutants manage administrative matters such as correspondence and keeping files secret as needed. Combat engineer officers lead enlisted marines out in the field doing demolition and construction work, such as building bridges when responding to natural disasters. The communications officer who oversees the radio and data systems operators is also responsible for communications planning, installation, operation, and upkeep, including on the battlefield.

COMMAND ELEMENT

The command element is the brains behind a mission. The people in this element form the headquarters. They devise the missions marines undertake.

Some MOSs are in the fields of intelligence, legal services, personnel, and public affairs. Public affairs MOSs specialize in media. For example, an enlisted marine in this field might work as a combat correspondent, gathering and creating information about the corps for military and civilian news outlets. A public affairs officer specializes in advertising the corps, writing articles and publishing newspapers on the branch's bases.

MUSICIANS, TOO

The marine corps also has a musical program. The US Marine Corps Musician Enlistment Option Program provides musicians who want to serve their country the opportunity to train as fighters and use their musical skills. Horn, percussion, and guitar are a few of the MOSs available in this category. Instrument repair technician is also an option.

The organization's music program is made up of the Marine Corps Bands and the US Marine Drum and Bugle Corps. In addition to performing at military ceremonies, these groups perform at concerts and parades

"THE PRESIDENT'S OWN"

The marine corps has a long musical history. In 1789, Congress established "The President's Own," a group of professional musicians who are also marines. The organization is a combination of the US Marine Band, the Marine Chamber Orchestra, and the Marine Chamber Ensembles. "The President's Own" performs frequently at the White House and beyond, with more than 500 public engagements nationwide annually.[5] "The President's Own" is the longest established professional musical organization in the nation. It has been continuously active since 1789.

The marine corps has many opportunities for musicians.

in civilian communities. The musical marines entertain audiences with music from a variety of genres. They also promote patriotism, particularly through songs such as "The Marines Hymn" and marches by famed composer and marine John Philip Sousa.

WOMEN IN THE MARINES

Women have been part of the marine corps since the early 1900s. Women were initially assigned to desk duty, but today's female marines fill roles their early counterparts could only have dreamed of.

Female marines serve in 93 percent of MOSs—all fields except combat arms, such as artillery, infantry, and tanks.[6] However, a few have taken part in infantry training. And while women do not fight in combat areas, they do serve in them.

Women in the corps also serve as officers. In 2011, the marine corps made Loretta E. Reynolds, a brigadier general, the first female to command recruit training at Parris Island, South Carolina.

MARINE CORPS RESERVE

Being part of the US Marine Corps does not require a full-time commitment. The marine corps describes its reserve as "for those who have both the willingness to raise their hand when our nation calls and the desire to

FIRST FOR FEMALES

Julia Carroll, Katie Gorz, and Christina Fuentes Montenegro made history in November 2013, becoming the first female marines to graduate from the corps' infantry training school. Training lasted 59 days and included completing a 12.5-mile (20 km) march through woods while carrying 85 pounds (39 kg).

The trio graduated with 221 men who immediately became part of infantry units.[7] The women, however, did not. Because women are not allowed to fight in combat areas, Carroll, Gorz, and Montenegro will take other jobs approved for women. However, the marine corps will make note of each woman's successful training in her record with the branch. Because they cannot take part in combat, women have fewer career opportunities in the marine corps. The Department of Defense wants ground combat service to be an option for women by 2016. If and when the opportunity arises, Carroll, Gorz, and Montenegro will be ready to take on the role.

pursue educational, career, and family goals in the civilian world."[8]

Reservists enlist for eight years. Just like regular recruits, reserve marines go through boot camp and are trained in an MOS. Reservists must train one weekend each month and two additional weeks each summer. After this, they serve in the Individual Ready Reserve (IRR). During this time, they no longer have to take part in marine corps life unless the corps specifically asks them to do so. Essentially, reservists are on call during IRR.

Reservists can also be officers. The requirements for reserve officers are the same as for officers in the regular corps.

In return for their commitment, the marine corps pays reservists and offers them educational assistance. Unlike regular marines, reservists are frequently assigned to units near their home. This allows them to be with their families and stay in their communities.

LEATHERNECKS, JARHEADS, AND DEVIL DOGS

Marines are known by other names. The nickname "leatherneck" comes from early uniforms, which had a rigid collar made of leather.

"Jarhead" comes from the hairstyle male marines wear. The name "describes the appearance of one's ears standing out after a very short haircut."[9]

Teufel Hunden, or "devil dogs," started in World War I. As the story goes, the Germans believed the marines were fierce fighters and called them the name. However, the story is only legend, and the spelling is incorrect. The correct German spelling is Teufelshunde.

Regardless of his or her choice of regular or reserve corps, a marine gains something immeasurable. The marine corps notes in a brochure for its music program, "Whatever path Marines choose for their futures, they know they have what it takes to be capable, quality citizens, confident leaders, and responsible individuals, forever committed to both country and community."[10]

CHAPTER NINE

LIFE IN THE MARINES

Joining the marine corps requires a commitment of at least a few years of active duty. Some marines serve longer. For example, officers commissioned from the US Naval Academy serve at least five years. As a member of the corps—or any military branch—the risks of service are obvious. Being sent into battle can result in injury

Marines gain courage and confidence through their training and service.

and even death. For those who join the corps, serving also has numerous benefits. In addition to physical and survival training, the US Marine Corps offers its members perks many civilians receive, including a salary, medical coverage, and vacation. The corps also provides housing, education, and travel.

But marines receive even more from and for their service. They become physically fit. And they gain a confidence in themselves and each other that lasts a lifetime.

SALARY AND BENEFITS

The marine corps pays its members a salary based on rank and experience. Depending on rank, in 2013 a marine earned between $1,516.20 and $19,566.90 each month.[1] Pay grows with experience, rank, and as a result of cost-of-living increases. Members also receive money for uniforms.

The marine corps provides health coverage to marines, as well as to their spouses and children. This includes full medical insurance at no cost. Those who make a career of the corps and actively serve for at least 20 years get a pension and retirement benefits. This means someone entering service at age 18 can retire at age 38 and have another career of 20 or more years as a civilian—all while having the financial and health benefits provided by the marine corps.

HOUSING

The marine corps provides on-base housing and requires new members to reside there. Living together creates a bond between marines and helps build the camaraderie required of service. Some on-base housing is for families, which allows couples and their children to be together.

MARINE CORPS RANKS

Enlisted

Private
Private First Class
<----------- Lance Corporal
Corporal
Sergeant
Staff Sergeant
Gunnery Sergeant
Master Sergeant
First Sergeant
Master Gunnery Sergeant
Sergeant Major ----------->
Sergeant Major of the Marine Corps

Officers

Warrant Officer
Chief Warrant Officer 2
Chief Warrant Officer 3
Chief Warrant Officer 4
Chief Warrant Officer 5
Second Lieutenant
First Lieutenant
Captain
Major
<---------- Lieutenant Colonel
Colonel
Brigadier General
Major General ---------->
Lieutenant General
General

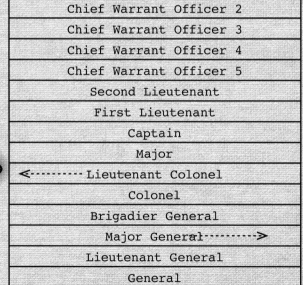

Living on base is similar to living off base. A base has places for worship, shopping, and schools and day care facilities for children. There are many options for things to do when not on duty. Marines may go bowling, visit a movie theater, or go out to eat—all on base. Because fitness is important, many marines start the morning with a run.

Living off base is also an option. Doing so requires approval. Those who live off base receive a monthly stipend to help with living expenses.

GUIDED BY MUSIC

While a marine corps base offers housing and elements of life similar to the civilian world, it has key differences. Music guides daily life, with loudspeakers playing bugle recordings to mark certain activities. Reveille wakes up marines early, often at 5:30 or 6:00 a.m. A second tune sounds mealtimes. And a third melody is played at colors, when the US flag is raised in the morning and lowered at sunset.

EDUCATION

Joining the marine corps automatically means learning at least one special skill through an MOS. Marines can also take advantage of education benefits.

While actively serving, a marine may pursue a college degree. A few options are available to help pay for textbooks, uniforms, and tuition and fees. Financing options include tuition assistance, the Post 9-11 GI Bill, and the Marine Corps College Fund, or the College Degree

Program. Officers in the corps already have at least an undergraduate degree. They can pursue a master's degree with help from the marine corps. Education benefits for officers are available after active duty and can even go to a marine's spouse or child.

Some officers take advantage of the Advanced Degree Program. Participants get an 18-month leave from the corps so they can be full-time students. Marine officers in the program continue to receive their pay and stipends. They do pay tuition themselves. However, as with enlisted

MARINES BY THE NUMBERS

Decade	Number of Marines	
	Beginning	End
1800s	368	523
1820s	685	895
1840s	950	1,076
1860s	1,851	2,384
1880s	1,968	1,772
1890s	1,772	3,142
1900s	3,142	9,696
1910s	9,696	48,834
1940s	19,432	85,965
1950s	85,965	175,571
1960s	175,571	309,771
1970s	309,771	185,250
1980s	185,250	196,956
1990s	196,956	171,154
2000s	171,154	204,153[2]

marines pursuing a college education, the GI Bill may cover some education costs.

TRAVEL

Serving in the corps is ideal for people who want to experience different places and peoples. Marines travel all over the world and experience a variety of cultures. In addition to basic training on the East or West Coast of the United States, a marine can be stationed in Europe, Africa, South America, the Middle East, or the Pacific.

Some assignments are on established marine bases. A marine might be stationed at Camp Pendleton for a year. Located near San Diego, California, its proximity to the ocean provides warm winters and opportunities for surfing.

Marines are proud to do their duty.

Other assignments are in government locations such as US embassies. An MSG might experience places, peoples, and languages as varied as those in Colombia, Morocco, and Russia.

Still others go wherever needed when a crisis strikes. Imagine flying to places demolished by nature's fiercest forces, seeing people in dire need of the most basic supplies, and helping them recover after such terrible loss. While the corps is a military branch, marines have opportunities to see and do much more than combat.

MORE THAN MONEY

The corps also offers intangible benefits. It instills in its members a confidence and camaraderie unlike any other. They must believe in themselves and one another to succeed. By simply becoming marines, they have done what many others have not and could not. And those who serve in the corps do so proudly.

The US Marine Corps was born out of conflict, and marines have been called on repeatedly to defend their country—and others—for more than 200 years. Those who serve may do so for a few years or for an entire career. Regardless of their time in active duty, these men and women are marines for life: "Once a marine, always a marine."[3] And they would have it no other way.

TIMELINE

1775

The Continental Congress approves formation of the Continental marines on November 10.

1798

The US government formally creates the United States Marine Corps on July 11, making it part of the US Navy.

1805

The marines win the Battle of Derna in Tunisia.

1847

In September, as part of the Mexican-American War, the US Marines win control of the National Palace, or Halls of Montezuma.

1908

President Theodore Roosevelt issues an executive order on November 12 specifying roles for the corps.

1918

In June, 8,000 marines defeat German troops in the Battle of Belleau Wood, stopping Germany from occupying Paris, France.

1918

On August 13, Opha Mae Johnson becomes the first female to enlist in the marine corps.

1945

Marines claim Mount Suribachi on the island of Iwo Jima on February 23.

1949

In September, marines begin training in racially integrated units.

1954

President Dwight D. Eisenhower dedicates the US Marine Corps Memorial on November 10.

2002

The corps begins using the new MARPAT camouflage.

2013

Julia Carroll, Katie Gorz, and Christina Fuentes Montenegro become the first females to graduate from the corps infantry training school in November.

ESSENTIAL FACTS

DATE OF FOUNDING
November 10, 1775

MOTTO
Semper fidelis
(Always faithful)

PERSONNEL (2013)
182,945 enlisted
21,208 officers
204,153 total

ROLE
The US Marine Corps is the military's expeditionary force. It specializes in quick deployment to conflict and disaster zones.

SIGNIFICANT MISSIONS
American Revolution, 1775–1783
Battle of Derna, 1805
Battle of Belleau Wood, World War I, 1918
Battle of Iwo Jima, World War II, 1945
Chosin Reservoir, Korean War, 1950

WELL-KNOWN MARINES

John Philip Sousa, bandleader and composer of military marches

Samuel Nicholas, first head of the Continental marines

First Lieutenant Harold Schrier, leader of the platoon that climbed Mount Suribachi on Iwo Jima

Corporal John F. Mackie, first marine to receive the Medal of Honor

Major Bill Hendricks, founder of Toys for Tots

Brigadier General Loretta E. Reynolds, first woman to command recruit training at Parris Island, South Carolina

QUOTE

"Some people spend an entire lifetime wondering if they made a difference in the world. Marines don't have that problem."—*Ronald Reagan, US president, 1981–1989*

GLOSSARY

AMPHIBIOUS
Operating on both land and water.

BAYONET
A fighting knife attached to a rifle and used to kill attackers.

DRONE
An aircraft that does not have a pilot on board but is directed by remote control.

EMBASSY
The residence and offices of an ambassador in a foreign country.

ENLISTED
A member of the armed forces who is not a commissioned officer.

EXPEDITIONARY
Sent to perform military service on foreign soil.

MAGAZINE
A piece of a gun that holds ammunition.

MILITARY OCCUPATIONAL SPECIALTY
The role or job a member of the armed forces has or does.

PRIVATEER
A private ship that attacks other ships with the approval of a government; a sailor who works on such a ship.

PUGIL STICK
A long stick or pole with padding.

REVEILLE
A bugle call, usually signaling morning.

SHOT
The ammunition used in cannons and antique weaponry.

SHRAPNEL
One or more of the pieces of metal from a bomb or mine that has exploded.

STALEMATE
A contest or battle in which neither side is a clear winner.

TOURNIQUET
A bandage or strip of cloth for tying tightly around a wounded arm or leg to slow or stop bleeding.

UNFURL
To unfold.

ADDITIONAL RESOURCES

SELECTED BIBLIOGRAPHY

Hammel, Eric. *Iwo Jima*. Saint Paul, MN: Zenith, 2006. Print.

Martin, Iain C., ed. *The Greatest US Marine Corps Stories Ever Told: Unforgettable Stories of Courage, Honor, and Sacrifice*. Guilford, CT: Lyons, 2007. Print.

Turley, Patrick. *Welcome to Hell: Three and a Half Months of Marine Corps Boot Camp*. Palisades, NY: Chronology, 2012. Print.

FURTHER READINGS

Dolan, Edward F. *Careers in the US Marine Corps*. New York: Benchmark, 2009. Print.

White, Ellen Emerson. *Into No Man's Land: The Journal of Patrick Seamus Flaherty, United States Marine Corps, Khe Sanh, Vietnam*. New York: Scholastic, 2012. Print.

WEBSITES

To learn more about Essential Library of the US Military, visit **booklinks.abdopublishing.com**. These links are routinely monitored and updated to provide the most current information available.

PLACES TO VISIT

ARLINGTON NATIONAL CEMETERY

Arlington, VA 22211

877-907-8585

http://www.arlingtoncemetery.mil

Visit the graves of thousands of men and women who have served the United States in one of its armed forces, including the marine corps.

NATIONAL MUSEUM OF THE MARINE CORPS

18900 Jefferson Davis Highway

Triangle, VA 22172

877-635-1775

http://www.usmcmuseum.com

Explore the history of the US Marine Corps at war-specific exhibits, learn what goes into making a marine, and see the Marine Corps Memorial.

US NAVAL ACADEMY MUSEUM

Preble Hall, 118 Maryland Ave.

Annapolis, MD 21402

410-293-2108

http://www.usna.edu/Museum/index.htm

View two floors of information about naval history, including how the academy develops officers for the marine corps.

SOURCE NOTES

CHAPTER 1. RAISING THE FLAG

1. James Bradley. *Flags of Our Fathers*. New York: Bantam, 2000. Print. 202–204.

2. H. Avery Chenoweth and Brooke Nihart. *Semper Fi: The Definitive Illustrated History of the US Marines*. New York: Main Street, 2005. Print. 239.

3. "What Are the Marine Corps Values?" *HQMC.marines.mil*. US Marines, n.d. Web. 20 Mar. 2014.

4. Iain C. Martin, ed. *The Greatest US Marine Corps Stories Ever Told: Unforgettable Stories of Courage, Honor, and Sacrifice*. Guilford, CT: Lyons, 2007. Print. 153.

5. "Battle for Iwo Jima, 1945." *Navy Department Library*. US Navy, n.d. Web. 20 Mar. 2014.

6. Ibid.

7. "Quotes: 1945." *Marines.com*. US Marine Corps, 2013. Web. 20 Mar. 2014.

8. H. Avery Chenoweth and Brooke Nihart. *Semper Fi: The Definitive Illustrated History of the US Marines*. New York: Main Street, 2005. Print. 14.

9. Wayne Hintze and Jerry Lehnus. "Recognition of Military Advertising Slogans Among American Youth." *IJOA.org*. Independent Job Analysis, 15 Oct. 2011. Web. 20 Mar. 2014.

10. "Selected USMC Slogans." *Heritage Press International*. Heritage Press International, n.d. Web. 20 Mar. 2014.

11. "US Marine Corps War Memorial." *NPS.gov*. National Park Service, 11 Jan. 2014. Web. 20 Mar. 2014.

CHAPTER 2. BIRTH OF THE CORPS

1. Chester G. Hearn. *An Illustrated History of the United States Marine Corps*. London, UK: Salamander, 2002. Print. 12.

2. Ibid. 13.

3. Ibid. 13.

4. Ibid. 13.

5. Jack Murphy. *History of the US Marines*. Greenwich, CT: Bison, 1984. Print. 18.

6. H. Avery Chenoweth and Brooke Nihart. *Semper Fi: The Definitive Illustrated History of the US Marines*. New York: Main Street, 2005. Print. 14.

7. "Reestablishment of the Marine Corps." *Navy Department Library*. US Navy, n.d. Web. 20 Mar. 2014.

CHAPTER 3. THE 1800S

1. Allan R. Millett. *Semper Fidelis*. New York: Free, 1991. Print. 44.

2. "US Forces Land at Vera Cruz." *History.com*. A&E Television Networks, 2014. Web. 20 Jan. 2014.

3. H. Avery Chenoweth and Brooke Nihart. *Semper Fi: The Definitive Illustrated History of the US Marines*. New York: Main Street, 2005. Print. 64.

4. Ibid. 18.

5. Ibid. 66.

6. Ibid. Print. 81.

7. Ibid. Print. 16–17.

8. "Legacy Walk: 1866–1914: First to Fight—The Age of Expansion." *USMCmuseum.com*. National Museum of the Marine Corps, n.d. Web. 7 Jan. 2014.

9. "The First Marine to Receive the Medal of Honor." *Marines.com*. US Marine Corps, 2013. Web. 20 Mar. 2014.

CHAPTER 4. THE 1900S

1. Linda D. Kozaryn. "Marines' First Crucible: Belleau Wood." *Defense. gov*. US Department of Defense, 18 June 1998. Web. 20 Mar. 2014.

2. "History of the Women Marines." *Women Marines Association*. Women Marines Association, 2013. Web. 20 Mar. 2014.

3. H. Avery Chenoweth and Brooke Nihart. *Semper Fi: The Definitive Illustrated History of the US Marines*. New York: Main Street, 2005. Print. 136.

4. Ibid. 277.

5. Ibid. 252.

6. Iain C. Martin, ed. *The Greatest US Marine Corps Stories Ever Told: Unforgettable Stories of Courage, Honor, and Sacrifice*. Guilford, CT: Lyons, 2007. Print. 92.

7. H. Avery Chenoweth and Brooke Nihart. *Semper Fi: The Definitive Illustrated History of the US Marines*. New York: Main Street, 2005. Print. 300–301.

8. Ibid. 303.

9. "Battle of the Chosin Reservoir." *Encyclopædia Britannica*. Encyclopædia Britannica, 2014. Web. 20 Mar. 2014.

10. "Meet the Montford Point Marines." *Marines.com*. US Marine Corps, 2014. Web. 20 Mar. 2014.

11. Ibid.

12. "History." *Montfordpointmarines.com*. Montford Point Marine Association, 2006. Web. 20 Mar. 2014.

13. "Missions: 1950: Chosin Reservoir." *Marines.com*. US Marine Corps, 2014. Web. 20 Mar. 2014.

14. "Operation SHUFLY Commemoration." *Marine Corps Gazette*. Marine Corps Association, Apr. 2002. Web. 20 Mar. 2014.

15. "Vietnam War." *Encyclopædia Britannica*. Encyclopædia Britannica, 2014. Web. 20 Mar. 2014.

16. H. Avery Chenoweth and Brooke Nihart. *Semper Fi: The Definitive Illustrated History of the US Marines*. New York: Main Street, 2005. Print. 375.

17. "1983 Beirut barracks bombings." *Encyclopædia Britannica*. Encyclopædia Britannica, 2014. Web. 20 Mar. 2014.

18. "Persian Gulf War." *Encyclopædia Britannica*. Encyclopædia Britannica, 2013. Web. 20 Mar. 2014.

19. Iain C. Martin, ed. *The Greatest US Marine Corps Stories Ever Told: Unforgettable Stories of Courage, Honor, and Sacrifice*. Guilford, CT: Lyons, 2007. Print. 284.

20. "Casualties: US Navy and Marine Corps." *History.Navy.mil*. National History & Heritage Command, 22 Feb. 2010. Web. 20 Mar. 2014.

21. "US Military Casualties—Operation Enduring Freedom (OEF) Casualty Summary by Casualty Category." *Defense Casualty Analysis System*. US Department of Defense, 20 Mar. 2014. Web. 20 Mar. 2014.

22. "US Military Casualties—Operation Iraqi Freedom (OIF) Casualty Summary by Casualty Category." *Defense Casualty Analysis System*. US Department of Defense, 20 Mar. 2014. Web. 20 Mar. 2014.

CHAPTER 5. THE MARINE CORPS' MISSIONS

1. H. Avery Chenoweth and Brooke Nihart. *Semper Fi: The Definitive Illustrated History of the US Marines*. New York: Main Street, 2005. Print. 427.

2. Ibid.

3. Ibid. 454.

4. "Structure." *Marines.com*. US Marine Corps, 2013. Web. 20 Mar. 2014.

5. "Chronological History of the Toys for Tots Programs." *Toys for Tots*. Toys for Tots Foundation, 2012. Web. 20 Mar. 2014.

6. Gina Harkins. "Marines Wind Down Efforts in Philippines. *Marine Corps Times*. Marine Corps Times, 30 Nov. 2013. Web. 20 Mar. 2014.

7. "First to Fight." *Marines.com*. US Marine Corps, 2013. Web. 20 Mar. 2014.

8. "National Impact." *Marines.com*. US Marine Corps, 2013. Web. 20 Mar. 2014.

9. "Your Impact." *Marines.com*. US Marine Corps, 2013. Web. 20 Mar. 2014.

CHAPTER 6. GETTING THE JOB DONE

1. H. Avery Chenoweth and Brooke Nihart. *Semper Fi: The Definitive Illustrated History of the US Marines*. New York: Main Street, 2005. Print. 476.

2. "Summary of the DOD Fiscal Year 2014 Budget Proposal." *US Department of Defense*. US Department of Defense, n.d. Web. 20 Mar. 2014.

3. "United States Marine Corps: America's Expeditionary Force in Readiness." *HQMC.marines.mil*. US Marine Corps, 17 Oct. 2013. Web. 20 Mar. 2014.

CHAPTER 7. BECOMING A MARINE

1. "Timeline." *Marines.com*. US Marine Corps, 2013. Web. 20 Mar. 2014.

2. "Basic School." *Marines.com*. US Marine Corps, 2013. Web. 20 Mar. 2014.

3. "Service Options: Enlisted." *Marines.com*. US Marine Corps, 2013. Web. 20 Mar. 2014.

4. H. Avery Chenoweth and Brooke Nihart. *Semper Fi: The Definitive Illustrated History of the US Marines*. New York: Main Street, 2005. Print. 27.

5. "Principles & Values." *Marines.com*. US Marine Corps, 2013. Web. 20 Mar. 2014.

CHAPTER 8. CAREER OPPORTUNITIES

1. "M4." *Marines.com*. US Marine Corps, 2014. Web. 20 Mar. 2014.

2. "Roles in the Corps." *Marines.com*. US Marine Corps, 2014. Web. 20 Mar. 2014.

3. "United States Marine Security Guards: Safeguarding American Missions around the World." *State.gov*. US Department of State, Bureau of Diplomatic Security, Nov. 2013. Web. 20 Mar. 2014.

4. Suzanna Knotts. "Training Unleashed: Marine Dog Handler Shares Bond with Canine." *Marines.com*. US Marine Corps, 29 Oct. 2013. Web. 20 Mar. 2014.

5. "The President's Own." *Marines.mil*. US Marines Corps, n.d. Web. 20 Mar. 2014.

6. "History of the Women Marines." *Womenmarines.org*. Women Marines Association, 2013. Web. 20 Mar. 2014.

7. Fabien Tepper. "First Female Marines Pass Infantry Training–But No Combat Yet." *CSMonitor.com*. Christian Science Monitor, 21 Nov. 2013. Web. 20 Mar. 2014.

8. "Marine Corps Reserve." US Marine Corps pamphlet. Author's collection.

9. H. Avery Chenoweth and Brooke Nihart. *Semper Fi: The Definitive Illustrated History of the US Marines*. New York: Main Street, 2005. Print. 17.

10. "United States Marine Corps Music Program." US Marine Corps pamphlet. Author's collection.

CHAPTER 9. LIFE IN THE MARINES

1. "2013 Military Pay Scale Chart—Effective January 1st, 2013." *MilitaryFactory.com*. MilitaryFactory.com, 2014. Web. 20 Mar. 2014.

2. "Decade Timeline." *Marines.com*. US Marine Corps, 2013. Web. 20 Mar. 2014.

3. "Once a Marine Always a Marine." US Marine Corps pamphlet. Author's collection.

INDEX

ABOUT THE AUTHOR

Rebecca Rowell has authored books for young readers on a variety of topics, including pop singer and songwriter Pink, education advocate Malala Yousafzai, pioneer aviator Charles Lindbergh, Switzerland, weather and climate, and wildfires. One of her favorite parts of writing is doing research and learning about all kinds of subjects. As the daughter and sister of three very proud marines, she was excited to write this book and is thankful to now better understand some of the experiences of her father and brothers in the corps. Rebecca has a master's degree in publishing and writing from Emerson College and lives in Minneapolis, Minnesota.